PHILLIP MARGULIES

Epidemics
Deadly Diseases
Throughout History

CREUTZFELDT-JAKOB DISEASE

The Rosen Publishing Group, Inc.
New York

Published in 2004 by The Rosen Publishing Group, Inc.
29 East 21st Street, New York, NY 10010

First Edition

Library of Congress Cataloging-in-Publication Data

Margulies, Phillip.
Creutzfeldt-Jakob disease / by Phillip Margulies.
    p. cm. — (Epidemics)
Summary: Traces the history, current issues, and future of Creutzfeldt-Jakob Disease, a rare genetic disorder that affects the brain and is part of the same group of illnesses as "mad cow disease."
Includes bibliographical references and index.
ISBN 0-8239-4199-X (library binding)
1. Creutzfeldt-Jakob disease—Juvenile literature.
[1. Creutzfeldt-Jakob disease. 2. Brain—Diseases. 3. Diseases.]
I. Title. II. Series.
RC394.C83 M375 2003
616.8'3—dc21

                                  20021524190

Manufactured in the United States of America

Cover image: An image of a human brain afflicted with subacute spongiform encephalopathy.

CONTENTS

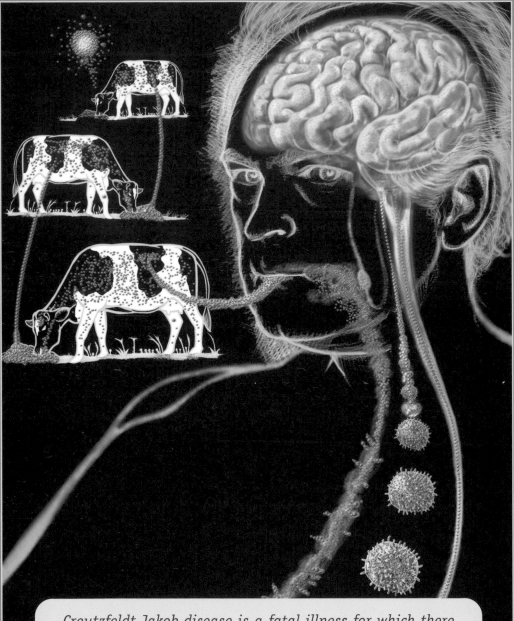

Creutzfeldt-Jakob disease is a fatal illness for which there is no known cure.

INTRODUCTION

Illness is one of the most challenging conflicts in life. It can strike us at the most unexpected times. It can also force us to rearrange our lives in ways we could have never imagined. Whether it is our own illness or that of someone we love, it is the biggest challenge most of us will ever need to face. And Creutzfeldt-Jakob (CROYTZ-felt YAK-ob) disease (CJD) is one of the most difficult.

Anne, whose name has been changed for this book, was a retired businessperson who worked part-time as a school crossing guard. She had been married for forty-four years and had nine children. Her family considered her to be an intelligent, strong-willed woman who paid attention to detail and took care of her health.

At age sixty-four, she exercised regularly, walking six miles a day. But one day on one of her walks, a dog attacked her. She fell to the pavement and suffered a severe blow to the head. X rays showed that she had fractured a vertebra in her spine.

A few weeks later, she began to suffer from symptoms that doctors attributed to her fall. Vision problems developed, which soon worsened to the point where she was no longer able to see well enough to drive a car. The doctors diagnosed her problem as "nerve palsy of the eye" and treated it by simply prescribing glasses.

But one of Anne's children, who was a nurse, worried that her mother's vision didn't seem to be improving. Talking it over with her sister, she learned of her mother's other symptoms. Anne was unsteady on her feet and often stumbled. In addition, she was losing her memory. Her daughter also learned a fact that Anne hadn't yet told her doctors: CJD existed in their family. Anne didn't mention this because she knew there was no cure and was afraid that if anyone found out, they would give up on her.

Of course, no one gave up on Anne. Her children hoped that she did not have this terrible illness, but they couldn't ignore the evidence that she might have it. They persuaded her to see a neurologist. Her daughters told her they would let the neurologist know that CJD ran in their family, but they would make sure that he and the other physicians tested her for every other possible cause for her symptoms. In any case, when a disease is considered to be incurable, it's standard practice for doctors to test for all the curable—or at least treatable—diseases that might have the same symptoms.

As it turned out, Anne did have Creutzfeldt-Jakob disease. Soon she went from needing a walker to needing a wheelchair. Her eyes no longer focused normally, so that she seemed to look through people. She began to have jerky movements in her hands, arms, and legs. Eventually, she became as helpless as a baby. Her children decided to take care of her at her home, assisted by hospice care—nursing help for people who are dying. They took turns keeping her company and helping to take care of her. About four months after her fall, Anne died.

In light of these facts, the mystery of Anne's illness was easier to understand. She wasn't sick because of her fall. On the contrary, she had fallen because she was sick. The attack by the dog was a red herring, a coincidence that had misled almost everybody. The only one who hadn't been misled was Anne. She had suspected the truth all along, but she had been afraid of what it meant.

What Anne's family didn't know was that CJD was a much larger problem than they could have ever imagined. And because of this, they would ultimately need to ask themselves questions that would affect the rest of their lives.

1

A MYSTERIOUS EPIDEMIC

Creutzfeldt-Jakob disease attacks the human brain by a mysterious process that science has only recently begun to understand. Under a microscope, the brain of someone who has died from CJD looks like a sponge because it is full of holes. This is because CJD attacks the brain of its victim, at first slowly, then at an increasingly faster rate.

As the damage to the brain spreads, patients lose more and more of their functions. The symptoms are numerous. Usually, they begin with the inability to sleep, problems with balance, loss of concentration and memory, and blurred or clouded vision. Patients then quickly lose the power to speak, walk, or take care of themselves altogether, usually dying within six months of the first symptoms. Medical researchers are working toward treatments for CJD, but as of now, the disease has a death rate of 100 percent.

One comforting fact is that Creutzfeldt-Jakob is rare. The odds of getting it are very low. In the United States, for example, only about two hundred people are diagnosed with CJD each year. Most are between fifty and seventy-five years old. Except for the small percentage of people who inherit the disease, there is no way of knowing whom it will strike.

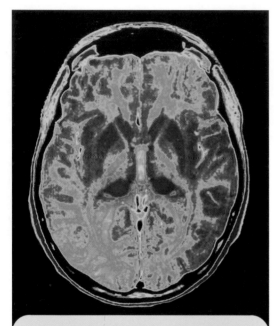

A magnetic resonance imaging (MRI) scan of the brain of a teenager suffering from CJD

The Gene for CJD

A predisposition to a disease can run in families. Like other inherited features, some diseases are passed down to us through our DNA (deoxyribonucleic acid), which is the blueprint for the body and is present in the nucleus of each of our cells. Composed of genes in what is called genetic code, DNA gives all living beings their characteristics. Height, weight, and skin color, among many other physical features and personality traits, are passed along from one generation to the next through DNA.

Because genes carry a wealth of information about a person, genetic testing has become a popular development in medicine. It's a powerful tool to help us predict if we will someday catch a disease that is passed through the genes. But by giving us this kind of advance knowledge, it puts some difficult choices into our hands.

The moral issues raised by genetic testing can be difficult to untangle. If you carry a gene for a disease as terrible as CJD, which you might pass on to your children, should you adopt children rather than have ones of your own? Should you avoid having children at all? Should you become emotionally close to people, knowing you'll eventually have to tell them the truth about your possible illness? What kind of life insurance policy should you buy for yourself to protect your family? How will learning about CJD affect the personal relationships you currently have? Will the knowledge that you have the genes for CJD weaken your relationships or make them stronger?

Another option to consider for people who have CJD genes in their family is to not be tested at all. After all, just because CJD is in a person's genes doesn't mean that he or she will contract the disease. Some people would live more comfortably simply not knowing whether they are going to live full healthy lives or if they are going to have their lives cut short.

Several days after her death, Anne's genetic test confirmed that she did, in fact, carry the gene for CJD, which meant that she inherited the disease. This posed troubling questions for her children. Did they inherit the CJD gene from their mother? Anne's disease had taken its course, but they had to now decide whether to take the test themselves. But did they really want to know that one day they might have a terrible incurable disease? How would they go on with their lives? Or would they rather live without the burden of knowing the facts? These were questions all of Anne's children would eventually need to answer for themselves.

Ways of Getting Creutzfeldt-Jakob Disease

There are several different ways of contracting Creutzfeldt-Jakob disease, just as there are several ways of getting a cold or flu. But with CJD, the methods of transmission each have their own names. This is because the way CJD is passed from one person to the next is an important factor in preventing its spread and potentially discovering a cure. Despite the different names, they are all the same disease. The symptoms and side effects are ultimately all the same. The only difference is how the disease is transmitted.

Iatrogenic Transmission

The word "iatrogenic," from the Greek, means "passed on by a physician or surgeon." The word is used to describe cases in which doctors have accidentally infected their patients with a disease. Infection occurs because a medical procedure directly exposed a patient to diseased tissue. For example, in the past, some people who had corneal transplants (a transplant of the cornea of the eye) developed CJD because the corneas they received had been taken from cadavers of people who had died from CJD themselves. People who had brain surgery have also been infected with the disease as well as people who were treated with human growth hormone that came from the pituitary glands of CJD carriers.

Doctors might also unintentionally infect their patients with CJD by using an instrument previously used to operate on CJD carriers. The problem, it is now known, is that the sterilization methods that work for most infectious agents don't always work for the ones that cause CJD. Though it is scary to think

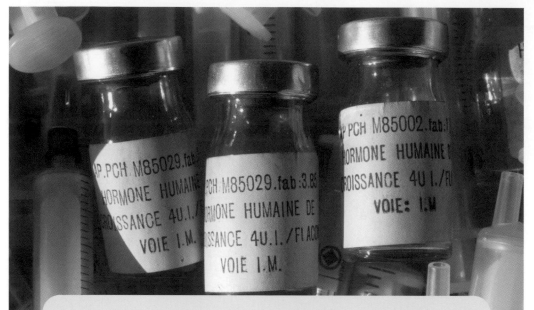

Pictured here are flasks of growth hormone contaminated with Creutzfeldt-Jakob disease (CJD).

that the disease can be transmitted so easily this way, scientists believe that iatrogenic transmission makes up less than 1 percent of CJD cases.

Familial Transmission

Familial CJD describes cases of the disease that are inherited, or passed down through the family, hence the name "familial." Though physicians can tell if a patient has the familial form of CJD by genetic testing, whether to have this test done is a difficult decision to make, as we saw in the case of Anne's children. On the one hand, getting the test done will let them know if they are at higher than average risk for getting the disease. While no effective treatments are available now for CJD, there may be in the near future, so this knowledge could save people's lives. Even if it doesn't, it could help them plan for the future.

On the other hand, many people are afraid of knowing the potentially devastating truth, considering that 10 to 15 percent of CJD cases turn out to be familial.

Sporadic Transmission

Sporadic CJD is the most common category. Between 80 and 85 percent of CJD cases are classified as sporadic, and the frightening part is that scientists do not know how or why these particular people get the disease. One day, perhaps soon, we might know more. But at the moment, there is no pattern to the sporadic cases other than the fact that they tend to occur in people who are more than fifty years old.

The diagnosis for sporadic CJD is usually made only after other diseases have been ruled out. When the CJD diagnosis has finally been made, either before death or after, doctors hunt for clues in a patient's history that might explain what happened. They try to find out whether anyone else in the family has had the disease. They might also do genetic testing; if the results are positive, they classify the case as familial. If the patient came down with CJD sometime after having brain surgery, a corneal implant, or some other medical procedure that has been known to lead to CJD, they classify the case as iatrogenic. If they can find no reason why the patient contracted CJD, doctors classify the case as sporadic.

Incubation Periods

Every disease has an incubation period—the time that passes between infection and the appearance of symptoms. Most diseases have short incubation periods. For example, people who catch a cold start sneezing a few days after they are infected. Other illnesses, like tuberculosis, have much longer incubation periods. A person might be infected with tuberculosis for years before becoming sick enough to know it. CJD has one of the longest incubation periods of any disease—between twelve and thirty years—which makes CJD extremely difficult to track.

When a disease has a short incubation period, it can be easy to track down the source of the illness. A man who has a cold remembers shaking hands last week with someone who had the sniffles. A woman suffering from food poisoning remembers something that tasted a little funny at the family picnic. But the person who contracted a disease that takes years to show its signs will have a more difficult time figuring out what caused it—and so will that person's doctors.

CJD in the Limelight

Rare diseases like Creutzfeldt-Jakob aren't usually regarded as a serious threat to public health because they affect a small percentage of the overall population. But lately CJD has received a lot of attention. One reason for this is public alarm about variant CJD (vCJD), a disease similar to regular CJD, which is part of the transmissible spongiform encephalopathy (TSE) family of diseases.

One example of vCJD is bovine spongiform encephalopathy (BSE), more commonly known as mad cow disease, a TSE that mainly affects cattle. BSE has received a lot of press lately. We now know that people can catch vCJD by eating the beef of cattle that have been infected with mad cow disease. Although the number of people who have caught a vCJD such as mad cow disease is very small, the idea that a fatal brain disease can be contracted by eating beef is frightening.

Today, most scientists agree that CJD is part of the TSE family. Patients suffering from vCJD show many symptoms similar to those of regular CJD, but there are noticeable differences as well. Regular CJD almost always afflicts people over fifty years of age. Variant CJD, on the other hand, typically affects young people, including teenagers and people in their twenties.

A technician at a pathology laboratory in Edinburgh, Scotland, prepares a microscope slide of brain tissue that will be tested for new variant Creutzfeldt-Jakob disease (vCJD).

Also, vCJD affects other parts of the body, such as the spleen and appendix, whereas regular CJD attacks only the brain. The brain waves of regular CJD patients, which are monitored by a machine called an electroencephalograph (EEG), look different from those of vCJD patients. Both are usually abnormal, indicating a loss of brain functionality, but they are abnormal in different ways, so much so that only a neurologist can tell them apart. Autopsies have shown that the brains of vCJD victims have, in addition to spongelike holes, other formations called plaques. Both the spongelike holes and the plaques severely hamper the brain's ability to function normally.

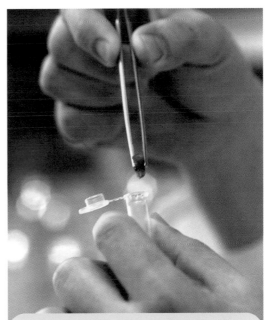

A researcher at the University of Zurich in Switzerland takes a close look at a piece of human brain tissue for traces of CJD.

Because of the long incubation period of vCJD, it's difficult to know precisely how many people might already be infected. To cope with the threat of the disease, governments have changed their agricultural and economic policies. Most countries now ban the importation of beef from the United Kingdom, where most cases of mad cow disease have occurred.

CREUTZFELDT-JAKOB AND MAD COW DISEASE

The first signs of mad cow disease were noticed in 1984 by a veterinarian inspecting sick cows at Pitsham Farm in South Downs, England. Since the animals' symptoms were so unusual, the veterinarian assumed the disease was undiscovered until then, and so he called it Pitsham Farm syndrome.

Two years later, pathologists discovered that Pitsham Farm syndrome belonged to the transmissible spongiform encephalopathy family of diseases. By then the first human cases of vCJD disease had been identified. Doctors concluded that the disease had been contracted by the consumption of meat from cattle infected with mad cow disease.

Naturally, the public was alarmed. Agricultural authorities in the United Kingdom took steps to slaughter infected cattle. Countries all over the world passed regulations banning the importation of beef from Great Britain.

To date, mad cow disease is believed to have taken the lives of approximately two hundred thousand cattle and one hundred human beings. Scientists now understand that the disease can be prevented by simply eliminating meat products from the cattle's feed.

2

THE HISTORY OF CREUTZFELDT-JAKOB DISEASE

In a scientific paper published in 1920, a young Austrian physician named Hans Gerhard Creutzfeldt (1885–1964) wrote about a patient he had seen some years earlier. He described her as delirious, uninterested in her surroundings, and suffering from numerous tremors in her body. Eventually, her breathing became so labored that she died only two months after reporting her first symptoms. Doctors were certain that some type of brain disorder was responsible for her death, but they were confused as to which one.

So the doctors conducted an autopsy. They found extensive damage to the nerve cells of the woman's brain, but no inflammation, which puzzled them. Usually, with this amount of damage, the body's immune system fights back, causing the tissues in the damaged area to become inflamed. The lack of inflammation showed the doctors that this woman's immune system had not even attempted to combat the disease. In other words, her body didn't even know the disease was there.

At about the same time, another Austrian physician, Alfons Maria Jakob (1884–1931), witnessed a series of similar cases, which he described in four medical papers published between 1921 and 1923. Jakob was convinced he was seeing a disease that had not yet been recognized. In one paper, he mentioned Creutzfeldt's earlier case, suggesting that his and Creutzfeldt's patients had the same illness. And so, the disease was eventually named after its two discoverers.

As other cases of CJD appeared, physicians began to acknowledge it as a distinct disease. In the years since its first discovery, CJD has been well tracked, but the understanding of its causes has come only slowly.

The Spread of Creutzfeldt-Jakob Throughout History

Scientists who track the prevalence of a disease are called epidemiologists. These specialists look at where and when a disease appears, searching for clues that can help them figure out what causes a disease and how it spreads. Epidemiologists studying CJD have found that it is distributed evenly throughout the population. There are a few exceptions, however, and these exceptions have given scientists important clues about the nature of this mysterious disease.

In Slovakian families and among Israeli families from Libya and Tunisia, cases of the disease have been found to be one hundred times higher than average. There has also been an extremely high incidence of CJD found in a large German family that immigrated to the United States at the beginning of the twentieth century. A case study done of the family by the National Institute of Neurological Disorders and Stroke (NINDS) found that nine family members had died of the disease. Two died while the study was being conducted. Research done on these clusters of CJD carriers helped scientists realize that the disease could be passed from one generation to the next and learn which specific genes were responsible.

Other dramatic CJD outbreaks have been iatrogenic, caused mostly by the medical use of tissue from cadavers that have been infected with the disease. While iatrogenic cases of CJD have a rare occurrence, they have resulted in the most publicized outbreaks. One case of iatrogenic CJD occurred in 1974 when a

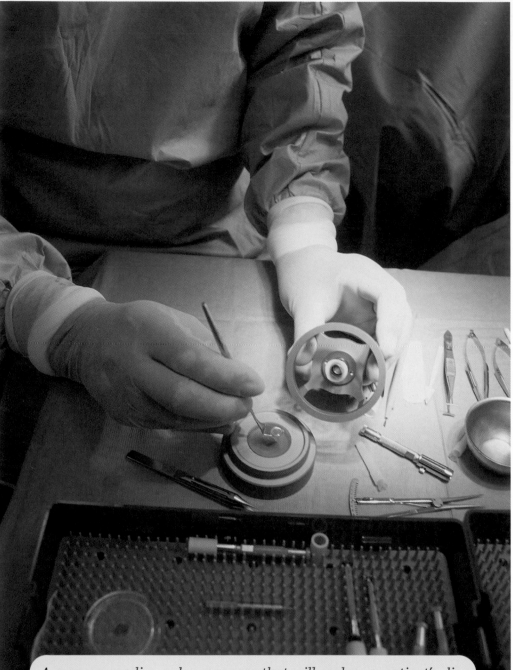

A surgeon readies a donor cornea that will replace a patient's diseased cornea during a surgical procedure called keratoplasty. This was the procedure blamed for a 1977 outbreak of CJD.

patient contracted the disease following a corneal transplant. Another patient who received a corneal transplant came down with the illness in 1977. Scientists later discovered that the corneas these people had received came from cadavers of people who had died from CJD.

In the 1980s, the U.S. Centers for Disease Control and Prevention (CDC) and the Food and Drug Administration (FDA) began investigating cases of the disease. Several people, it turned out, had shown symptoms shortly after having brain surgery in which they had received grafts, or transplants, of human tissue called dura mater, a protective lining of the brain, which

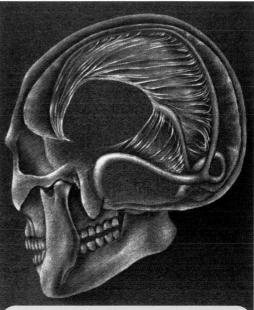

This drawing depicts the dura mater, tissue that lines and protects the human brain.

often needs to be replaced after brain surgery. All the grafts had come from cadavers, and all had been prepared by the same company. Researchers believe that one or more of the cadavers were those of people who had died from CJD. The dura mater from the cadavers had been stored with other dura matter, which infected the entire batch. Since 1988, more than seventy people who received grafts during neurosurgery have died from Creutzfeldt-Jakob.

But of all the causes of iatrogenic infection, the use of human growth hormone has been the most common. Growth hormone is produced by the pituitary gland. Children and adults whose pituitary glands don't produce enough of the hormone need a source of extra growth hormone. Children who don't have enough growth hormone fail to grow. Adults who don't have enough gain weight and are more

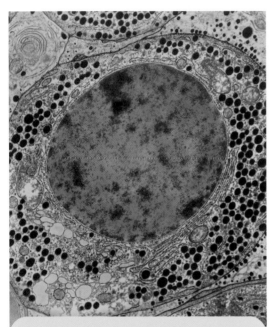

Pictured here is a somatotroph, a cell in the human body that secretes growth hormone.

likely than average to suffer from heart disease.

In the mid-1960s, manufacturers found a way of extracting growth hormone from the pituitary glands of cadavers. The pituitary glands that had been taken from the cadavers were thrown together in batches of up to ten thousand to produce the hormone, which was an accident waiting to happen. All it took was one unit of infected growth hormone to contaminate the entire batch.

And this is exactly what happened. In 1985, three people who had received human growth hormone contracted CJD and died. The hormone from the cadavers was immediately taken off the market and was replaced with an artificial version. Because of the long incubation period of CJD, however, new cases of CJD among people who had been treated with human growth hormone continued to appear over time— more than one hundred people have since died in France, Great Britain, and the United States as a result. Because of CJD's long incubation period, it is still unknown how many more cases of the disease will emerge from people who were infected this way in the past.

1921–1923
Six cases of CJD are described, one by Hans Gerhard Creutzfeldt and five others by Alfons Maria Jakob.

1974
Study shows high incidence (seventy-five per million) of CJD in Israel among Jews from Libya or of Libyan-Jewish descent. The cause is probably genetic in origin.

1975–2001
Twenty-two cases appear in Orava, Slovakia. This incidence of CJD is hundreds of times higher than the normal rate. The cause is probably genetic.

1974
The first case is found in the United States of CJD contracted after corneal transplant surgery.

1984 to present

Sixty-two people in France contract CJD after treatment with human grown hormone.

1987

A study shows a high incidence of CJD (eighteen per million) for inhabitants of central Chile.

2002

A twenty-two-year-old British woman living in Florida shows symptoms of variant Creutzfeldt-Jakob disease (vCJD).

1985 to present

Twenty-two people in the United States contract CJD after being treated with human growth hormone.

1988 to present

More than seventy people die from CJD in Britain, New Zealand, Italy, Japan, and the United States after receiving contaminated dura mater grafts during neurosurgery.

3

A FAMILY OF DISEASES

Today, many scientists agree that CJD is part of the TSE family. Animal diseases in the TSE family include scrapie, a disease of sheep; mad cow disease; transmissible mink encephalopathy (TME), a disease of mink; and chronic wasting disease (CWD), which appears in mule deer and elk.

In addition to CJD, TSEs that human beings suffer from include Gerstmann-Straussler-Scheinker syndrome, which is similar to CJD but strikes people at an earlier age and takes longer to become fatal; fatal familial insomnia (FFI), an extremely rare inherited disease that begins with severe insomnia and ends in death; kuru, a disease similar to CJD; and Alpers disease, which is also similar to CJD, but attacks infants.

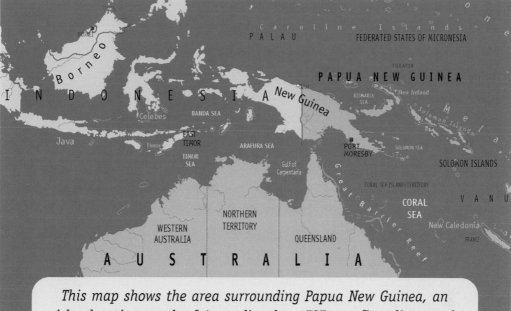

This map shows the area surrounding Papua New Guinea, an island nation north of Australia where TSE was first discovered in the indigenous Foré people.

Kuru in New Guinea

The first clues to the TSE family of diseases were found when scientists began to study a disease that afflicted a single group of people, the Foré of the eastern highlands of Papua New Guinea. One day a patrol officer in the Foré territory saw a young girl shaking violently with her head jerking from side to side. Talking to the Foré with the help of a Lutheran missionary, he learned that the girl suffered from a disease the Foré called *kuru*, which means "shiver and tremble." The fatal disease primarily affected children and young adult women and was widespread in Foré territory. Thousands of the Foré people were dying of the mysterious disease, which was unknown elsewhere in the world.

The first sign that someone might have kuru was usually a problem with coordination—the person would begin to stagger, which would become worse until the person could no longer walk without help. Finally, the person would no longer be able to stand. Many carriers died within nine months of the first symptoms appearing.

The Foré believed that kuru was caused by sorcery. For this reason and the fact that kuru did not match the symptoms of any other diseases they knew of, Australian doctors came to the conclusion that the illness must be psychosomatic. That is, they believed that the disease must not be a physical disease of the body, but rather, a psychological disease that existed in the minds of the carriers. The doctors concluded that the belief among these people that they had been cursed was so strong that not only did they have serious symptoms from kuru, but they also died from it.

Not all medical practitioners, however, believed that kuru was merely a psychosomatic illness. In fact, they found this explanation to be ridiculous. Too many people were sick and dying. There had to be a physical cause.

So, in 1957 a team of scientists traveled to Papua New Guinea to investigate the disease. The scientists studied every possible cause of kuru and, at first, were baffled. Diseases are usually caused by one of three factors: infectious agents, inheritance, or poor nutrition. Scientists could find no infectious agents. Neither could they find any signs that the disease was inherited. Though they suggested that malnutrition was responsible, the evidence didn't seem to point in that direction, either.

In one respect, however, the Foré diet turned out to be an important factor in the spread of kuru. A U.S. pediatrician by the name of Daniel Carleton Gajdusek noticed that the Foré had one very unusual eating habit— they practiced ritual cannibalism, or the eating of the flesh of other human beings. This was part of one of their most important religious rituals. When a member of the Foré died, eating the corpse was a part of the funeral ceremony.

Daniel Carleton Gajdusek receives the Nobel Prize in Stockholm, Sweden, in December 1976, for his work with kuru.

Many of the Foré believed that kuru was by caused by sorcerers (magicians). In fact, there were sorcerers among the Foré who cast spells in an attempt to inflict kuru. To cast the spell, the sorcerer collected personal objects connected to the intended person, such as discarded food, hair, or clothing. After collecting these items, the sorcerer bound the victim's possessions with crumbled stone and leaves and tied them together with vine. Then the sorcerer would beat the bundle with a stick while saying the words, "I break the bones of your legs; I break the bones of your feet; I break the bones of your arms; I break the bones of your hands; and finally, I make you die." Then, the bundle would be buried in muddy ground. As it rotted away, so did the person's health.

To combat the spells, the Foré, in effect, fought fire with fire. They used spells to fight off the spells that they believed caused the disease. They would try to find out which sorcerer had cast the spell and once they found him, they would force him to dig up the bundle. Sometimes they would have the sorcerer put to death.

Gajdusek suggested that cannibalism was the means by which the Foré caught kuru. He pointed out that the way the Foré divided the corpse for eating also explained why the Foré children and women were more prone to contracting the disease than the men. When the corpse was eaten, Gajdusek noticed, the men and more senior members of family took the choicer parts, the muscles. Young women and children were far more likely than men to be left with the organ meats, including the brain, where whatever caused kuru probably lived.

A Pattern Between Creutzfeldt-Jakob Disease and Scrapie

Gajdusek and his colleagues published their findings in 1957 and continued to study the disease. Two years later, in 1959, a U.S. veterinarian named William Hadlow, who had read Gajdusek's work, noted that scrapie, a disease of sheep, was strikingly similar to kuru in humans. Scrapie had been known in Europe since the eighteenth century, when wool became an important raw material because of the growth of the textile industry. Since sheep were the source of wool, diseases that sheep suffered from were of great concern. Scrapie was thought to be contagious among the herds. It was also believed that sheep could contract it from inbreeding, that is, from mating between members of the same family. Sheep suffering from scrapie had many of the same symptoms as human beings suffering from kuru, one of which was the same spongelike appearance of the brain.

The same year that Hadlow noticed the similarity between scrapie and kuru, a neuropathologist named

Federal agents in Vermont in 2001 collect sheep for quarantine that may have been afflicted with scrapie.

Igor Klatzo noticed a similarity between kuru and CJD as well. After dissecting the brains of twelve people who had died of kuru, Klatzo said that they resembled the brains of people who had died from CJD.

A Mysterious Agent

Through this work and the work of other scientists in the 1950s and 1960s, a medical consensus began to grow that Creutzfeldt-Jakob disease belonged to the TSE group of diseases.

Many puzzling questions remained, however. Though scientists had been able to prove that an

The outward signs of CJD are similar to the much more common disorder that was once called senile dementia and is now called Alzheimer's disease. The symptoms are so similar that many patients with CJD are sometimes mistakenly diagnosed with Alzheimer's. One of the first symptoms of both Alzheimer's disease and CJD is tiredness. In both diseases, people also lose their memory, speech, and the ability to control their movements. In addition, they may hallucinate, that is, see and hear things that aren't there.

A study conducted at Yale University found that as many as 13 percent of people who were thought to have had Alzheimer's disease had, in fact, died of CJD.

infectious agent of some kind could transmit CJD, the nature of that agent remained unknown. They assumed it was a virus because viruses were the smallest infectious agents known, and whatever caused CJD had to be small enough to have escaped notice for such a long time. Some scientists suggested that the cause must be a "slow virus," because there was such a long time between infection and the appearance of symptoms.

But in all the years since the discovery of CJD, no one has managed to find a virus that seems to cause it nor have they found a virus that can be proven to cause any of the other TSEs.

4

A CLUE

The whole family of TSE diseases presented scientists with a puzzle so baffling that even if a clue were found, many scientists would not believe the discovery. This is because the TSE diseases work very differently from typical infectious diseases.

Ever since the 1860s, when Louis Pasteur and Robert Koch first demonstrated that diseases could be caused by germs, scientists have held rigid ideas about contagious disease. Most infections are caused by microscopic organisms, organisms that—like the amoeba—are composed of only one cell. Many diseases, from streptococcal infection to botulism, are caused by bacteria. Others are caused by fungi, the class of organisms to which mushrooms belong. Many other diseases, from smallpox to the common cold, are caused by still smaller microorganisms called viruses.

Other contagious diseases are caused by relatively large organisms. One example is the worm that causes trichinosis in pigs, which human beings can catch by eating undercooked pork.

All this research left scientists mentally unprepared to understand TSEs, which behaved like no other disease agent yet discovered.

The Unkillable Infection

A common characteristic of all infectious agents is that they cause our immune systems to respond to them. When an invader attacks, the white blood cells in our bodies produce special proteins called antibodies to fight the infection.

Each infection brings about a particular type of antibody. Some of the discomfort that comes with illness—fever, runny nose, cough—aren't the result of the infection itself, but of the immune system trying to fight off the infectious agent.

But when scientists conducted autopsies on the animals that had contracted TSEs, they found no antibodies and no signs of the body's immune response. The immune systems of the animals and people with TSEs had failed to recognize that there was any

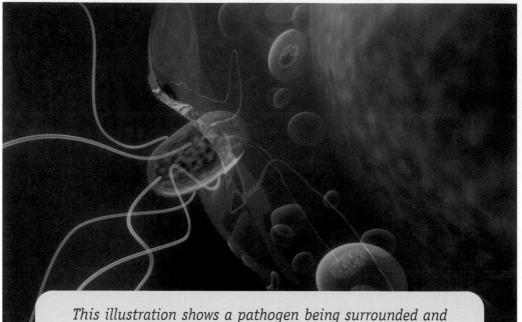

This illustration shows a pathogen being surrounded and neutralized by a white blood cell in the human body.

invader to fight. This lack of a response makes TSEs particularly difficult to fend off.

Another surprising characteristic of whatever was causing TSEs was that it was amazingly hard to kill outside the body. Neither alcohol nor hospital detergents did the job. Not even boiling would kill it off. Even radiation, which usually kills both bacteria and viruses by destroying their DNA, had little effect on TSEs.

Proteins Gone Wrong

An important clue to the cause of TSEs came in 1978 when a U.S. scientist named Pat Merz looked at the brains of scrapie-infected sheep under an electron microscope, a microscope that can magnify an object up to 100,000 times, making it possible to see organisms as small as viruses. Looking at scrapie tissue under these high magnifications, Merz saw hazy threads that did not appear in the tissue of healthy animals. Furthermore, Merz discovered that there was a direct correlation between how sick the animal was and the number of threads present in the brain. The further the disease progressed, the greater was the number of these threads. She wondered if these threads might be the disease agent that caused CJD, scrapie, kuru, and the other TSEs.

Acting on Merz's lead, other researchers identified these tiny strands as a protein molecule, the building block of the body. For some reason, this particular molecule had multiplied until it began taking over the brain. It was found in the brains of animals that suffered from TSEs, but it was not found in healthy brains.

One scientist who found this protein particularly fascinating was Stanley Prusiner. As a young doctor in 1972, Prusiner had treated a woman with Creutzfeldt-Jakob disease. He believed that the strange protein was not merely a symptom of CJD but was in fact its cause. As the disease progressed, these proteins made copies of themselves and spread through the brain, destroying nerve cells in their path.

Prusiner and his colleagues later called the abnormal protein PrP, short for prion protein. But how could something that contained no genetic material reproduce itself and spread throughout the brain, since the idea that a protein could reproduce itself went against the most basic assumptions of biology?

Dr. Stanley Prusiner and his colleagues identified the abnormal prion protein that causes CJD.

The Bad Protein

The idea that a protein could reproduce itself had been suggested before, however. While making photocopies of a scientific paper, Prusiner and his colleagues came across another paper on the subject of scrapie, which anticipated the results that their work was proving. It was published in 1967 by a mathematician named J. S. Griffith.

Griffith made a suggestion about the way a disease-causing protein could reproduce. Although he was not a biochemist, Griffith knew that protein molecules could have more than one structure and that the structure of a protein molecule is an important aspect of its ability to perform its job.

Suppose, said Griffith, that there were an abnormal protein, a version of a common protein that was structured the wrong way. He claimed that it was possible that this protein could bind to the surface of a normal protein and change its structure accordingly, making the normal protein abnormal as well. If this were to happen, one abnormal protein molecule would become two, two would become four, four would become eight, and so on. The number of abnormal proteins would mount faster and faster until they eventually became a serious threat to normal tissues. The conclusion that Griffith reached was that these abnormal proteins could have been causing the damage to the brains of people and animals that died from TSEs.

Prusiner had arrived independently at these conclusions, which were basically the same as Griffith's. He discussed his ideas about the cause of TSEs in a paper published in 1982 in which he found that there are two types of PrP in the brain. One is a normal protein common in all animals. Another is the disease-causing form of the protein, which Prusiner called "prion," a word that he derived from the name "proteinaceous infectious particle."

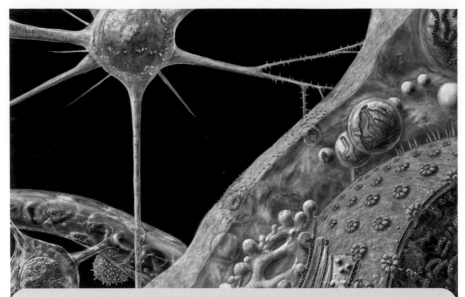

This illustration depicts what happens at the cellular level when prions (the round, purple objects) replicate and infest the normal proteins of the human brain.

A prion is chemically identical to the original protein. The only difference is their structures. Like normal proteins, prions can link up in long chains. Normally the body breaks down unneeded proteins, but the unusual shape of prions lets them resist this process. Meanwhile, they turn normal proteins into prions at a very rapid rate, killing brain cells and creating the holes in the brain that are characteristic with CJD victims.

The Gradual Acceptance of Prion Theory

As more research is done, an increasing number of scientists have come to believe the prion theory.

One reason for this growing acceptance of the theory is simply that despite intensive research, no one has been able to find any other agent that might cause TSEs.

Scientists have been using the term TSE to describe a group of mysterious diseases whose symptoms were similar, but whose causes were unknown. But as time goes on and prion theory takes hold, this term is being used less often. Increasingly, the diseases that used to be classified under the name TSE are now called prion diseases.

5

THE FUTURE OF CREUTZFELDT-JAKOB DISEASE

CJD is still a rare disease. Public health officials sometimes call it an orphan disease. An orphan disease is defined by the Orphan Drug Act of 1983 as a condition affecting fewer than two hundred thousand Americans. Under this definition, there are six thousand orphan diseases. Many orphan diseases affect only a few thousand people. Some affect even less. A disease called Sakati syndrome, which causes malformation of the head, face, hands, feet, legs, and heart, has been found only once, in one Saudi Arabian boy in 1971. Other orphan diseases such as cystic fibrosis, muscular dystrophy, and hemophilia can affect hundreds of thousands of people.

What all the orphan diseases have in common is that they don't affect enough people to make a profitable enough market for drug companies to conduct research for new drugs. They tend to attract far less money for research and drug development than a major epidemic such as cancer or heart disease. Sadly, they often receive less attention than even the common cold from drug manufacturers looking for a profitable market.

Patients who come down with orphan diseases also have many other problems in common. Rare diseases tend to go unrecognized by doctors who don't specialize in them, so for 35 percent of patients with orphan diseases, diagnoses take, on average, from one to six years. In 15 percent of cases, diagnoses take more than seven years. And once they're diagnosed, patients with orphan diseases must often travel long distances to find doctors who specialize in their disease. The cost of diagnosis and treatment for a rare disease can reduce the patient's family to poverty.

Well, one might think, at least this isn't a problem that affects many of us, since orphan diseases are, by definition, rare. Oddly enough, this isn't true—while each orphan disease is rare, when you add all six thousand of them, they're not rare at all. An orphan disease will strike one in ten Americans in their lifetime.

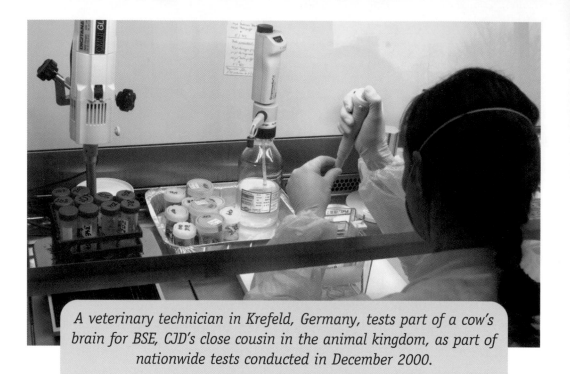

A veterinary technician in Krefeld, Germany, tests part of a cow's brain for BSE, CJD's close cousin in the animal kingdom, as part of nationwide tests conducted in December 2000.

Taken together, orphan diseases are the most common and most costly health problem in the United States.

Although the research into CJD has not yet led to a cure or even a treatment, CJD is an exception among orphan diseases. Because of mad cow disease and because of the unusual nature of the prion puzzle, CJD has received a great deal of attention. Two Nobel Prizes have been awarded for research into CJD and its family of diseases—something that cannot be said of the vast majority of the thousands of diseases classified as rare. In fact, the scientific revelations that CJD research has produced are often cited as an example of the way research into rare diseases can repay the effort put into them. Thanks to earlier research on CJD, kuru, and scrapie, public health officials were able to realize quickly what was causing vCJD and to take steps to avert a more widespread epidemic.

In addition, fear of vCJD continues to fuel research into regular CJD. Scientists realize that preventing mad cow disease does not mean that the threat of vCJD has been eliminated. If, like regular CJD, vCJD has a long incubation period, people might be getting sick for years to come. No one knows how many more cases of vCJD may show up in people who ate infected meat as far back as ten or twenty years ago. Can we expect an epidemic to occur at some time in the future? This dire possibility continues to spur further research into the cause, treatment, and cure of CJD.

Current Research

Stanley Prusiner, who received a Nobel Prize in 1997 for his research into the abnormal proteins that cause CJD, believes that a therapy for CJD and the other prion diseases may be available early in the twenty-first century. He cautions, however, that there is still much that is unknown about the way prions lead to disease.

A small portion of CJD cases—those caused by infection with prions from the tissue of other CJD sufferers—are preventable. Using what is known now about CJD, public health officials are taking steps to eliminate the transmission of the iatrogenic form of the disease. Scientists are also trying to find drugs to slow down the spread of prions and to find a vaccine to prevent infection in the first place. In addition, scientists are trying to better understand the disease process and establish better ways of diagnosing the illnesses.

Though at present there is no treatment, early diagnosis will be very helpful when a treatment is found.

New Ways of Diagnosing Creutzfeldt-Jakob Disease

Until recently, the only certain way of knowing that a person had CJD was by performing an autopsy. This has since changed. Recently, German scientists developed a test that detects prions in cerebrospinal fluid, which is found around the brain and spinal column where it functions as a shock absorber. This test uses antibodies to carry a fluorescent dye to the prions, if there are any. A highly focused laser beam scans the sample and detects the fluorescent molecules. This procedure is a great improvement in determining whether a person died of CJD, but is little use to living patients since the test is done only after symptoms appear.

Researchers at the Serono Pharmaceutical Research Institute in Switzerland are working on techniques that might lead to a blood test for CJD. Ordinarily, the blood of a CJD patient contains too few proteins to detect. The Swiss researchers use ultrasound (high-frequency sound waves) to break up clumps of proteins, thereby exposing more proteins to any prions present in the blood and hastening the speed at which the prions turn good proteins bad. Soon

A researcher records results from a blood test. Detecting CJD through blood testing is currently being explored by Swiss scientists.

the number of prions becomes large enough to detect. The ability to detect very small amounts of prions that are present in the blood can lead to a blood test for prions, which means a blood test for

CJD infection. As of 2002, however, this research is still in its early stages.

Drugs to Stop CJD

In the talk he gave at the University of Pennsylvania in 2002, Stanley Prusiner pointed to two promising new drugs that might help stop the spread of the prions that cause CJD. The names of these drugs are quinacrine, used to treat malaria, and chlorpromazine, used to treat schizophrenia and other psychoses.

Researchers believe these drugs help stop normal proteins from converting into disease-causing prions. Recently, quinacrine and chlorpromazine were tested on patients with vCJD and patients with sporadic CJD. The drugs succeeded in reducing the symptoms early in the treatment but failed to cure the disease.

Although these drugs did not effectively treat CJD—much less cure the disease—the research at least showed that drugs can interfere with the spread of prions and slow down the process. Prusiner and other researchers want to continue to investigate quinacrine and chlorpromazine and also to investigate other drugs in search of more effective treatments for CJD. Their study will include as many as eleven thousand drugs.

A Vaccine?

Meanwhile, scientists are exploring the possibility of developing a vaccine for prion diseases, including CJD. Some scientists have doubted whether this is possible since prions don't seem to evoke an immune response from the body, and vaccines work by preparing the body's immune system to resist an invader before the invader appears.

Nevertheless, researchers at the New York University School of Medicine are exploring this approach. They've given a genetically engineered, nontoxic prion to experimental mice, which they've later infected with a prion disease. While the vaccine did not prevent the mice from contracting the disease, it did cause the mice to produce antibodies to fight the prions, and it succeeded in delaying the onset of the disease. It usually takes mice an average of 120 days to develop prion diseases. Those that had been given the vaccine took sixteen days longer to show signs of the disease.

These results are encouraging because they show that it is possible to encourage the immune system to respond to prions. Scientists feel that the fact that it took the vaccinated mice longer to get sick is at least a step in the right direction toward the cure for Creutzfeldt-Jakob disease.

GLOSSARY

Alzheimer's disease A brain disorder that usually
develops in men and women over age forty with
symptoms such as loss of memory, difficulties
speaking, and overall mental decline.

antibodies Proteins made by the body's immune
system to attack and destroy foreign substances,
such as bacteria and viruses.

autopsy A surgical examination performed on a
body to determine the cause of death.

bacteria Extremely small one-celled organisms
that usually have a cell wall and multiply by
cell division.

cerebrospinal fluid A fluid within the brain and
the spinal cord that cushions the brain around

the skull and protects the spinal cord from mechanical shocks.

contract   To become infected with.

cornea   The outer, clear, round structure that covers the colored part of the eye (iris) and the pupil.

correlation   A relationship between things or events that could not be expected based on chance alone.

deoxyribonucleic acid (DNA)   The molecule that is the basis of heredity. It contains the coded instructions for reproducing an organism.

electroencephalograph (EEG)   Machine that records electrical impulses from brain activity, detected by means of electrodes attached to the outside of the skull.

epidemiologist   A scientist who tracks the prevalence or spread of disease.

fungus   Plants that lack chlorophyll, including molds, rusts, mildews, smuts, mushrooms, and yeasts.

gene   A hereditary unit that is composed of a sequence of DNA.

hallucinate   To have visions or imaginary perceptions.

iatrogenic   Caused by physicians.

incubation period   The interval between the time a person catches a disease and the time that symptoms begin to appear.

kuru A brain disease affecting the Foré people of Papua New Guinea. It is similar to Creutzfeldt-Jakob disease.

neurologist A doctor specializing in disorders of the nervous system.

nucleus The center of all cells; The nucleus contains DNA and other materials that are essential for life.

outpost A military base; an outlying or frontier settlement.

parasite An organism living in or on an organism of another species that does not benefit its host.

prion A "proteinaceous infectious particle" or abnormal form of a protein. A prion is identical to its normal counterpart except for its shape. It does not contain DNA or RNA.

protein An organic molecule used by plants and animals to build structures.

scrapie A brain disease that occurs in sheep.

sporadic Unpredictable or random.

toxic Poisonous.

transmissible spongiform encephalopathy (TSE) A group of degenerative brain diseases that affects animals and human beings and that includes Creutzfeldt-Jakob disease.

validity   The degree to which a fact or statement is well grounded or justifiable.

virus   Microbe consisting of a core of RNA or DNA enclosed in an outercoat of protein. Viruses can live and reproduce only in the host cells of other organisms.

FOR MORE INFORMATION

Centers for Disease Control and Prevention (CDC)
Office of Health Communication
National Center for Infection Deseases
Mailstop C-14
1600 Clifton Road
Atlanta, GA 30333
(404) 639-3311
(800) 311-3435
Web site: http://www.cdc.gov

Creutzfeldt-Jakob Disease Foundation, Inc.
P.O. Box 5312
Akron, OH 44334
(330) 665-5590

(800) 659-1991
Web site: http://www.cjdfoundation.org

National Institutes of Health (NIH)
9000 Rockville Pike
Bethesda, MD 20892
(301) 496-4000
Web site: http://www.nih.gov

In Canada

Calgary Health Region
Communications
10101 Southport Road SW
Calgary AB T2W 3N2
(403) 943-5465
Web site: http://www.calgaryhealthregion.ca/
    hlthconn/items/cjd.htm

Health Canada
A.L. 0900C2
Ottawa, ON K1A 0K9
(613) 957-2991
Web site: http://www.hc-sc.gc.ca

Web Sites

Due to the changing nature of Internet links, the Rosen Publishing Group, Inc., has developed an online list of Web sites related to the subject of this book. This site is updated regularly. Please use this link to access the list:

http://www.rosenlinks.com/epid/crjd

FOR FURTHER READING

Debre, Patrice, and Elborg Forster. *Louis Pasteur*. Baltimore: Johns Hopkins University Press, 1998.

DeSalle, Rob. *Epidemic! The World of Infectious Disease*. New York: The New Press, 1999.

Karlen, Arno. *Man and Microbes: Disease and Plagues in History and Modern Times*. New York: Simon & Schuster, 1996.

Klitzman, Robert. *The Trembling Mountain: A Personal Account of Kuru, Cannibals, and Mad Cow Disease*. New York: Perseus Books, 2001.

Newton, David. *Sick! Disease and Disorders, Injuries and Infections*. Fourth ed. New York: UXL, 2000.

Rhodes, Richard. *Deadly Feasts: The 'Prion' Controversy and the Public's Health*. New York: Simon & Schuster, 1997.

INDEX

CREDITS

About the Author

Phillip Margulies is a freelance writer who lives in New York City.

Photo Credits

Cover and chapter title interior photos, Dr. F. C. Skvara/Peter Arnold, Inc.; pp. 4, 44 © Russell Kightley Media; p. 10 © S. Fraser/Photo Researchers; p. 14 © Fonlupt Gilles/Corbis Sygma; p. 18 © James King-Holmes/Science Photo Library; pp. 19, 48 © Reuters NewMedia/Corbis; p. 24 © Laurent/Photo Researchers; p. 25 © M. Pelnar/Custom Medical Stock Photo; p. 26 © Quest/Photo Researchers; p. 31 © GEOATLAS; p. 33 © AP World Wide Photos/Tobbe Gustavsson; p. 36 © AP World Wide Photos/Toby Talbot; p. 40 © Kenneth Eward/BioGrafix/Science Source/Photo Researchers; p. 42 © AFP/Corbis; p. 51 © Ken Glaser/Index Stock Imagery, Inc.

Designer: Evelyn Horovicz; Editor: Nicholas Croce